MEDICINAL HERBS AND
ESSENTIAL OILS

MEDICINAL HERBS AND
ESSENTIAL OILS

ANTHONY GARDINER

SELECT
EDITIONS

This edition published 1996 by the
Promotional Reprint Company Ltd
Kiln House, 210 New Kings Road
London SW6 4N2
for Selecta Book Ltd, Devizes, Wiltshire, UK

Copyright
Text © Anthony Gardiner and the Promotional Reprint Company Ltd 1995
Layout and Design © Promotional Reprint Company Ltd 1996

ISBN 1 85648 383 5

ACKNOWLEDGMENTS

Anthony Gardiner wrote the text used on pages 6-25 and 64 and provided the
photographs and captions. Cathy Cooper wrote the text for pages 26-63.

PUBLISHER'S NOTE

Neither the Publisher nor the Author take any responsibility for the implementation of
any recommendations, ideas or techniques expressed and described in this book. Any
use to which the recommendations, ideas and techniques are put is at the Reader's sole
discretion and risk.

Printed and bound in China

CONTENTS

The Place of Herbs in Modern Medicine

The main difference between conventional medicine and herbal medicine is in cause and effect. Modern, chemically-synthesised drugs help a doctor to treat ailments quickly by dealing with the effect rather than seeking the cause. A medical herbalist will treat a patient holistically, concentrating on the cause of the ailment and treating it accordingly.

Modern science and technology has made us believe that we can no longer help ourselves effectively. In many cases we have become lazy, relying on the expertise of professionals. Plant remedies have been gradually lost to us and, worse still, ridiculed as 'quack' remedies and 'country magic'. However, no one with any common sense is going to suggest that plants can heal in every case. Areas of modern medicine, take for example in the field of heart surgery and replacement surgery, could not hope to rely on the healing virtues of herbs. But in helping to promote a healthy lifestyle and general well-being, herbs have a rightful place in the home; and in the treatment connected with balancing the body and encouraging the healing process from within, qualified medical herbalists have every justification to take their place alongside modern medical scientists and practitioners anywhere.

Considering the thousands of years of research and practice in plant medicine it seems incredible that so much is still being discovered and waiting to be discovered. It is fascinating to think that only now can we begin to appreciate the complexity of plants, and so appreciate the good and bad effects they can have on our bodies.

For example, scientists in Scotland are now conducting research on the effect that thyme has on the ageing process, while evening primrose and feverfew are just two other herbs that have recently been the subject of lengthy scientific papers. The benefits of such research on nutrition and general health are available to us because of the efforts and enthusiasm of these scientists and technicians.

Many sceptical doctors are keen to point to the placebo effect whenever someone claims to have been helped by plant medicine. The Latin meaning of 'placebo' – 'I shall be acceptable or pleasing' – suggests an improvement in the patient's condition brought about solely by a belief that the treatment will work. But this theory of course also applies to orthodox medical treatments. Further, in controlled research done on cattle, who after all have no intelligent reasoning, the effect of homeopathic remedies in the treatment of mastitis was proven beyond all reasonable doubt by the administration of minute droplets of plant drug in drinking water.

Above: Double-flowering feverfew is a member of the daisy family grown for its decorative as well as curative properties.

Since medieval times the phrase 'everything in moderation' has applied to the use of herbal medicine as well as other areas of our lives. Another phrase, more in current use today, is 'less is more'. Because of the holistic nature of plant medicine, where the whole plant is used rather than an isolated constituent, then the natural balance of that plant comes into play. By increasing the amount of plant material, you do no more good than you would by increasing a dose of pills. In fact, if you take the latter course, you could totally upset the balance of your body and, in the end, cause far more harm than good.

It cannot be stressed enough that in the plant world, as in the animal world, there is bad as well as good. Always consult a good book or, better still, a qualified herbal or medical practitioner before embarking on any lengthy course of treatment.

The Development of Herbal Medicine

Evidence that early humans had an instinct about which plants could safely act as medicines came with the discovery of a Neanderthal burial site in Shanidar, Iraq. Pollen taken from wild flowers which had been placed around the bodies indicated the belief that these would be of use to the deceased on their journey through to the next world.

A similar belief by the ancient Egyptians that provision should be made for the after-life has allowed us more than just a glimpse into the art of medicinal herbalism. Plant remedies written on papyrus in Egypt and on oracle bones in China during the Yin dynasty (circa 1500BC) show a flourishing business in plant medicine. In ancient Greece, Hippocrates established a scientific school to study and investigate into herbal medicine, expounding the theory that healing came from within the individual, assisted by diet and massage, with herbal remedies used to restore the balance of the system. This was the first known reference to holistic medicine. The Romans continued the study further, but superstition and religious belief infiltrated medicinal recipes.

While Europe experienced what has come to be known – some would say erroneously – as the Dark Ages (roughly 476-1000AD) the Arab nations introduced the science of the pharmacy, and produced highly educated physicians trained by Avicenna, a Persian physician who turned the study of plant medicine into a science as well as an art. Proof of his genius is witnessed in the 'Unani Tibb' system of medical practice still seen in India today, which are taken from his teachings. With the rise of the monastic tradition in Europe, the study of Latin, Greek and Islamic texts gave rise to the practice and teaching of herbal medicine in all towns in which there were monasteries. By the time of Henry VIII (reigned 1509-1547), when, with the dissolution of the monasteries, the country was in danger of losing this tradition to only a handful of doctors, permission was granted by Royal Charter for all people to practise herbal medicine. So began the Golden Age of the Herbalists.

The writings that influenced the golden age of the 16th and 17th century herbalists arrived in Northern Europe by a very circuitous route. The first serious moves in the scientific study of herbs were begun by a Greek pupil of Aristotle called Theophrastus (born 370BC). His *Enquiry into Plants* listed over 500 species, with careful descriptions of each. In the main, these studies explore the plants growing in the Mediterranean region around Greece, but also include references to some species from Egypt.

Right: Feverfew is commonly known as a 'migraine' herb. Eat a leaf between pellets of bread every day to relieve the symptoms.

In 60AD an army physician, who was serving under the armies of Nero, prepared the definitive herbal of his age. It was called *Peri hulas iatrikes*, better known by its Latin name *De Materia Medica*. His name was Pedanius Dioscorides, and he came from Anazarba in Asia Minor. Each plant had a drawing and attached description, followed by medicinal information and adverse effects, if any. This herbal became the model for all future works up until the early 16th century. At about the same time Pliny the Elder produced his *Historia Naturalis* before dying while investigating the eruption of Vesuvius in 79AD

There now began a tug of war between the Islamic and Christian faiths, each intent on the advance of learning. Manuscripts captured in the Islamic wars against Byzantium were taken to the House of Wisdom in Baghdad. A vast amount of research was carried out, and teaching centres and pharmacies were set up as far afield as Spain. The medical school in Salerno, near Naples, became a centre for the study of plant medicine; and reputedly there was a library at Cordoba in the 10th century containing over 600,000 volumes on plants.

The Benedictine monasteries, established by St Benedict in the 5th century AD, evolved from the teachings of St Anthony, a hermit gardener in Fayum, Egypt. In the 9th century the monks drew up an ideal plan for a monastery at St Gall, near Lake Constance, in Switzerland. At this time too, Walafrid Strabo (meaning Walafrid-the-Squint-Eye), Abbot of Reichnau Abbey, also on Lake Constance, wrote his poem *Hortulus*, or *The Little Garden*. This delightful treatise, which went undiscovered for 600 years, sets out the manner in which the abbot created a herb garden from a wilderness. In the relative calm following the reign of Alfred the Great, two Anglo-Saxon herbals were written. They were: The *Leech Book of Bald* and the *Lacnunga*.

The *Leech Book*, written on stout vellum and miraculously still in existence at the British Library, begins: 'Bald is the owner of this book which he ordered Cild to write.' He was assisted by two Saxon doctors called Dun and Oxa, who supplied him with prescriptions. The book is a strange mixture of Christian ritual and superstition. Elves and goblins are much in evidence, and a number of remedies refer to being 'elf-shot', an affliction caused by the pricking of tiny arrows fired by aggrieved elves.

The *Lacnunga* is also steeped in magic and medicine and seems to concern itself a great deal with remedies for 'flying venom'. Meanwhile in Salerno a manual of preventative medicine was being written called *Regimen Sanitatis*. This was to lay the foundation for generations of medical herbalists. My favourite quotation from the book sums up the philosophy of common sense:

'If you want to stay hale and healthy, stop worrying about trifles, have a light lunch, and do not strain too hard at stools. If there are no doctors around, do not worry: the best doctors are a happy mind and moderation in all things.'

The first printed herbals

In 1476 William Caxton set up his first printing press in London. The first true herbal to come off the printing presses took another 50 years to appear. It was published by Richard Banckes, and although some scholars would suggest that it derived from an early medieval manuscript, it has all the hallmarks of an original work. In 1526, one year afterwards, there appeared *The Grete Herball*. This popular herbal was printed in Southwark by Peter Treveris, and used as its source a French herbal called *Le Grand Herbier*.

Both books are set out in the now-recognised style of the 'herbalis', or herb book. This has the names of plants with a description, and their properties and virtues. But the *Grete Herball* went even a stage further, including giving advice on how to avoid being duped by quack apothecaries. The reader was being let into the hidden 'secrets' of the herbalist, and the way was prepared for self-medication.

Above: The foxglove, *Digitalis purpurea,* must only be used under strict medical supervision.

Turner's herbal

In 1551 the publication of William Turner's *A New Herball* heralded the age of the classic herbals. From the popularity of this work Turner gained the well-deserved title of the Father of English Botany. It is, in every way, a completely original work that influenced all following herbals for ages to come.

Printed by Peter Cole
In Leaden-Hall

In Effigiem Nicholai Culpeper Equitis
croſs fecit in Aquafort

The ſhaddow of that Body heer you find
Which ſerves but as a caſe to hold his mind,
His Intellectuall part be pleas'd to looke
In lively lines deſcribed in the Booke.

Turner was born in Morpeth, Northumberland, during the reign of Henry VIII. Like many men to follow him he was what has since come to be recognised as a Renaissance man. Having studied divinity, he also became interested in medicine and plants, and was a physician and a botanist. His patron through university at Cambridge, and the man to whom he dedicated the second part of his herbal, was Thomas, Lord Wentworth. Turner says in his dedication: 'Wherefore I dedicate unto you this my litle boke, desyring you to defende it against the envious evil speakers, which can alow nothing but that they do themselves.' This second part of the herbal was published in Cologne, where Turner was living in exile during the reign of Queen Mary.

In 1558, at the accession of Elizabeth I, Turner returned to England and was reinstated in the deanery of Wells. He was a powerful preacher, but prone to non-conformist behaviour, the most frowned upon by his superiors being the incident when he trained a dog to snatch the square cap from his bishop's head. Soon after this he left Wells and settled back in London at Crutched Friars, where he had a notable garden. The third and final part of his great work was published in 1568, the year of his death, and dedicated to Queen Elizabeth in the firm belief that such a herb book was a right and meet gift for such a queen. The strength of his personality shines through on every page, whether he is eulogising about chamomile or chastising the superstitions surrounding the mandrake and those who sought to capitalise on it. This was the first British scientific study of more than 230 of our native plants with exceptional woodcuts by Fuchs.

Gerard's Herbal

The fact that John Gerard used Dr Priest's translation of Rembert Dodoen's work *Pemptades* without authority for the botanical descriptions of the herbs, doesn't spoil the enjoyment of this famous herbal one bit. Allowing for the justified criticism which this deliberate and blatant act of plagiarism has received, it is the personal observations and unique wit of Gerard that makes this one of the most enjoyable works of the Elizabethan age.

John Gerard was born at Nantwich in Cheshire in 1545. He was a professional plantsman, and delighted in any rare or unusual introduction brought to him. He grew over 1,000 plants in his garden in Fetter Lane, Holborn, where he prided himself particularly on his ability to grow even the most difficult of foreign plants. 'These be strangers in England, yet I have them in my garden, where they flourish as in their natural place of growing.'

Left: Nicholas Culpeper was an astrologer and apothecary who revolutionised health care for the poor people of Spitalfields. He wrote *The English Physician Enlarged* in 1653 as a guide to self-medication with herbs. This book has proved to be one of the most enduring herbals ever written and still one of the most popular in the world.

Gerard was well-respected by members of his profession, as is clear from his friendship with Jean Robin, keeper of the royal gardens in Paris. Of all the new vegetables being introduced into England at that time, he was one of the first to grow potatoes, which he refers to as the 'Virginia potato'. It has often been suggested that William Shakespeare was a friend of Gerard, as he lived close by to him, and the knowledge of herbs and wild flowers described in his later works in particular undoubtedly share some of the folk quality that Gerard explained so keenly. Certainly Gerard's Elizabethan prose is romantic and cultured in its execution. A brief extract from his preface can vouch for that:

'What greater delight is there than to behold the earth apparelled with plants as with a robe of embroidered works, set with Orient pearls and garnished with great diversities of rare and costly jewels? ...The principal delight is in the mind, singularly enriched with the knowledge of these visible things, setting forth to us the invisible wisdom and admirable workmanship of almighty God.'

The Herball was published in 1597 with well over 1,800 illustrations. However even these were to become the cause of some notable controversy. John Norton, the queen's printer, was given the loan of the woodcuts from a work called Eicones by Jacob Theodor published in 1590. Gerard used them to illustrate his text, but made so many mistakes with the descriptions that the Flemish botanist, Mattias de l'Obel, was brought in to do the corrections.

De l'Obel, no doubt out of professional zeal, claimed the need to do over a thousand alterations. Gerard settled the matter by declaring that de l'Obel had 'forgotten' the English language, and testified to its accuracy. De l'Obel never forgave Gerard for this insult to his professional pride, but it should be noted that it is John Gerard whose name we remember, and whose knowledge of plants was recognised as second to none. George Baker, a critical contemporary, wrote of a particular visit to Paris that Gerard

'was desirous to go abroad with some of our herbarists...when it came to the trial my French man did not know one to his fower.'

There certainly does appear to be a remarkably enigmatic quality to Gerard's character. We know very little about his life and personality, but we do get glimpses of a great deal of his charm, his humanity, his humour and his strength. His constant reference to plants that 'make men merry' points to an entertaining man you would just love to meet and pass time with.

Parkinson's Herbal

In 1640, John Parkinson's *Theatrum Botanicum* was published. He was 73 years of age. In this lengthy work over 3,800 plants are described. Parkinson's original intention was to name the book 'A Garden of Simples', which would have well described this treatise on all known medicinal plants. Somehow the *Theatrum Botanicum* failed to attract the popularity of one of his earlier works, *Paradisi in Sole – Paradisus Terrestis*. This was published in 1629 and his sense of humour is evident in the pun on his name, used in the title – 'Park in the sun'. He was well qualified to write a herbal on medicinal plants as he was apothecary to James I. He was also great friends with John Tradescant the elder, and shared the confidence of Charles I and his wife Henrietta Maria to whom he dedicates his *Paradisus*. Following publication of the book he was appointed Botanicus Regis Primarius to Charles I.

Parkinson's garden was in Long Acre, and he delighted in visiting other famous gardens nearby, in particular Master Ralph Tuggie's, where he claims he saw the 'most beautiful gillyflower,' which he 'needes therefore call "Master Tuggies Princesse" '. In his classification of plants into 'Classes or Tribes' he refers to 'Venemous Sleepy and Hurtfull plants and their Counter Poysons', 'Hot and Succory like Herbs', and the 'Unordered Tribe': a group of 'straglers that have either lost their rankes or were not placed in some of the foregoing orders that so I may preserve them from losse…'. I think we all have a group like that somewhere in our gardens.

Nicholas Culpeper

It is strange how out of adversity great things often transpire. When Nicholas Culpeper (1616-54) was at Cambridge University studying Greek and Latin, he and his fiancée planned to elope. On her way to meet him her carriage was struck by lightning and she was tragically killed. His academic life, in the comfortable, cloistered world of Cambridge, suddenly appeared a sham of luxury. Feeling desolate and embittered he left university and apprenticed himself to an apothecary in London, eventually setting up on his own among the desperately poor people of Spitalfields.

Having studied Latin he realised that it precluded everyone except the well-educated and the privileged classes. In 1649 he set about translating some of the learned works of the College of Physicians, to make them more accessible to the ordinary apothecaries. His first project was the *London Pharmacopoeia* (1649), in which he also pours contempt on those 'proud, insulting, domineering Doctors whose wits were born above five hundred years before themselves'. He was critical of high charges and the over-prescribing of drugs. Here was a man learned enough and skilled enough to administer drugs with care and, above all, drugs to suit the poorest purse. In educating the common people about the virtues of English herbs he quite logically listed them by common name, and commented on the practice of the College of Physicians of using only Latin descriptions:

'It seems the College hold a strange opinion, that it would do an English man mischief to know what the herbs in his garden are good for.'

Nicholas Culpeper was a remarkable man. An apothecary who practised as a doctor, a puritan and a Parliamentarian. He appears to be a socialist ahead of his time and was greatly scorned and vilified by the establishment. Unmoved by this criticism, Culpeper played his trump card and published *The English Physician Enlarged* in 1653. This followed the tried and tested path of his own experience as a herbal practitioner with an added dimension, that of astrology and its influence on the plant world:

'He that would know the reason of the operation of the Herbs must look up as high as the stars.'

This suggested 'quack' philosophy caused delighted uproar among the many hostile conventional practitioners who decried his work and his deep social sensibilities.

The English Physician was an immediate success and became a best seller. It still is. It has been published in more than 40 different editions. Perhaps Culpeper hit on the right formula, maybe it was just a herbal for his time, but one thing is certain: Nicholas Culpeper's unselfish devotion to the craft of herbal medicine, and his obvious 'common touch', has guaranteed his name will live for many more years to come. Sadly he died young, from tuberculosis, in 1654 at the age of 38, leaving a wife, Anne, and seven children.

Above: The entry on meadowsweet from Sowerby's Herbal published in 1826.

William Coles

Another theory taken up with zeal by William Coles in the 17th century was the doctrine of signatures - that the form of the herb reflects the part of the body it treats (so, pilewort roots look like haemorrhoids). It had been conceived by Paracelsus nearly 100 years earlier who stated: 'I have oft-times declared, how by the outward shapes and qualities of things we may know their inward Vertues, which God hath put in them for the good of man.' Sadly for William Coles his arguments found few followers after his death and his doctrine was repudiated as quackery.

The New Science and Beyond

With the invention of the printing press, the herbals of Gerard, Turner, Parkinson and Culpeper reached a wide market, and the use of herbal medicine flourished during years of plague and disease, ailments which were mostly exacerbated by overcrowded, insanitary cities. But in the late 17th century the discovery of 'New Science' began to change things dramatically.

Herbs such as Peruvian bark and sarsaparilla arrived from the New World, enabling doctors to treat specific ailments such as malaria and syphilis. Treatment of the whole body was abandoned in favour of treatment of the disease. By the middle of the 19th century orthodox medicine was overtaking herbal medecine and when a breakthrough in the creation of synthesised drugs occurred at the end of the century, scientists could isolate components of plants and manufacture drugs such as aspirin.

After World War 1 there was a serious shortage of drugs and people were encouraged once more to use herbal medecine for treating minor ailments. An upsurge in interest coupled with a wave of nostalgia for a more natural way of life led to the prominence of such women as Maude Grieve and Hilda Leyel educating an eager public in the virtues of plants. As a result of the work of the National Institute of Medical Herbalists (established in 1864), the Herb Society (set up by Hilda Leyel) and the emergence of properly qualified medical herbalists, the science of herbal medecine has not been lost to us.

There is, however, still a long way to go to an official recognition of herbal practitioners and sensible licensing of herb drugs. But research institutes, the Chelsea Physic Garden, Auchincruivre in Scotland, and schools of herbal medecine are all contributing to the furtherance of our knowledge and protection of a natural heritage which otherwise could so easily be lost.

Medicinal Uses of Herbs

Using Medicinal Herbs

There are many ways to make up herbal preparations, depending on your needs. The most common are: infusions - including tisanes and syrups - infused oils and creams and ointments. Others are: poultices and compresses, tinctures, vinegars and smoking mixtures.

Infusions and Tisanes

This is the most common form of medicinal treatment. It can be taken as a tea, or as a gargle, applied to the affected area as a douche or lotion, added to a bath or used for inhalation or fumigation. The method is quite simple. Simply pour 600ml/1pt of boiling water over 25g/1oz of dried herbs in a teapot and allow to infuse for up to 10 minutes. Then strain and drink. You can add honey to sweeten the tea. If you are using fresh herbs you will need to add more as they retain water. Always collect herbs in the early morning before the sun begins to warm them, but after the dew on them has dried.

For inhalations just pour boiling water over 5-10ml/1-2tsp of the herb in a bowl and place a towel over your head, breathing in the steam through your nose and breathing out through the mouth.

When using herb roots you will need to make a decoction. Again, use 600ml/1pt of water to 25g/1oz of herbs. Place in a tight lidded saucepan and simmer for about 10-15 minutes. Strain off the liquid, return it to the pan and, removing the lid, reduce to one third. This can then be turned into a syrup or kept in the fridge for a few days.

Syrups

Make a tisane, then slowly dissolve 350g/12oz of sugar to a syrup. Pour into well labelled, clean bottles.

Infused oils

The best method for this preparation is to use a water bath, or bain marie. Avoid using aluminium containers. If you do not have a water bath, then you can improvise by placing a small pan inside a larger one, resting the smaller pan on two spoons. Put water in the larger pan and place your herbs and oil into the inner pan. Use a tight lid.

Chop up your fresh herbs or roots and use 25g/1oz of your chosen herb to 600ml/1pt of oil. Almond oil is the best, but quite expensive. Grape seed oil is a good alternative and has the distinction of being odourless. Simmer for two hours and then strain off the oil and discard the herbs. Repeat the process with fresh herbs for another two hours.

The resulting oil is quite concentrated and is most effective as a massage oil and for putting in the bath.

Creams and Ointments

Take your infused oil and, using the same bain marie, add 25g/1oz of beeswax, stirring it in over a low heat. As soon as the mixture is well blended, pour it immediately into sterilised jars.

To sterilise jars and bottles, simply wash well and then dry in a low oven, or use Milton sterilising solution and dry as before.

Poultices and Compresses

Both poultices and compresses stimulate the skin by the use of heat and allow the herbs to be absorbed through the skin. Poultices are made with pulped vegetables made into a paste with mixed herbs plus a small amount of oil. Spread the mixture while hot between a double layer of cotton gauze, then lay it on the fine grill of a sieve and steam over boiling water. Compresses are ways of applying infusions and decoctions to the affected area. After soaking a cloth in the infusion, wring it out and apply at once to the injury.

Tinctures

I would recommend buying tinctures from a chemist or herbalist. Alternatively, consult a qualified herbal practitioner.

Vinegars

Vinegars have been used both internally and externally for many years. They are easy to make, and are ready to use within one week of preparing.

Right: Alchemilla vulgaris or Lady's mantle. The leaves and flowers are used to promote health in pregnancy and assist in an easy birth. Dew drops collected at dawn from the leaves are supposed to be particularly powerful.

Dilute water and vinegar in equal parts using cider or malt vinegar. Add a handful of herbs for every 600ml\1pt of solution. Place in a wide-necked jar with a screw-top lid and put in a dark place for at least one week. Turn occasionally. Strain off the herbs and pour into a clean and preferably sterilised bottle.

Smoking Mixtures

Smoking mixtures have been used for treating asthma and bronchial complaints. Simply mix your dried herbs with 5ml/1tsp of honey and 20ml/4tsp of water. Dry in the open for a few days and when it feels only slightly damp, store the mixture in air-tight containers.

Hazardous Herbs

A report in the newspapers in June 1990, highlighted the phototoxic effects of rue (*Ruta graveolens*) on the skin. The highly responsible article referred to a case where children playing with the flowers of plants in the garden on a hot, sunny day had broken out in painful blisters and brown stains. Doctors were baffled until the mother of one of the children took cuttings of the plants they had been playing with to the hospital. Now, some years on, there need be no more ignorance on the part of doctors regarding hazardous plants, as the Royal Botanic Gardens at Kew have developed a system called Plato (Plant Toxins – UK) which provides information at the press of a button on all poisonous and hazardous plants in the United Kingdom.

Before you go rushing out into your garden to tear out your rue, and any other hazardous plant, it is worth considering the true dangers of hazardous herbs. Certainly, not all herbs are 'safe': but very few are life threatening, and most of them are growing in the wild anyway..

Responsible organisations such as the Herb Trade Association police the labelling of their plants, and herbs such as rue are clearly labelled at the retailers with warnings about the effects they may have on some people. The fact that rue does not affect all types of skin is valid. Just as medicinal herbs do not necessarily work in the same way for every individual, then so it is with hazardous plants. Poisonous plants, however, do affect everyone in exactly the same way – and they are dangerous and must be treated with respect.

If you are in the habit of picking wild berries, or making tisanes from wild plants, it is as well to identify your plants very carefully indeed. The umbelliferal family in particular is an absolute minefield when it comes to poisons. Goutweed, wild angelica, hedge parsley, cow parsnip and sea carrot have a striking similarity to fool's parsley, wild chervil, hemlock and hemlock water dropwort. These last four plants are extremely dangerous. The great philosopher Socrates was put to death by being made to drink hemlock, so be warned.

Unless you choose to grow any of the above herbs in your garden you have little to fear; and even if you do have buttercup, columbine, foxglove, ivy, laburnum and yew there is no harm in growing them as long as you are aware that eating any part of them in large quantities is potentially harmful. There has been only one recorded fatality from any of these in recent years, and that was from laburnum seeds.

Be aware and take precautions, particularly if you have children who are naturally curious about plants. Begin to educate them about

Right: Henbane, *Hyoscyamus niger,* grows in sandy, waste places, very often near the sea. It is so toxic that its use in medicine is now severely restricted.

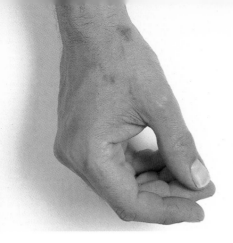

Above: An example of the blistering caused by rue, *Ruta graveolens*, on a sunny day. The blistering will eventually fade but can last for up to eight weeks.

which plants are harmful, and warn against eating any berries in the wild until they know exactly what they are. It would be a pity to deprive any child of the simple joys of blackberry picking.

The most common problems encountered in the garden are caused by skin contact with plants that cause allergic reactions. Common nettle rash or, urticaria, is caused by a chemical reaction, as is the sting from stinging nettles, or from a specific immune response, such as a specific reaction to certain types of vegetables or fruit.

Rue is not the only culprit when it comes to blisters. Apparently, beggars used to rub their faces with buttercups to make themselves look sick, in the hope that people would take pity on them. The phototoxic effect is caused by the reaction of ultra-violet (UV) rays from the sun on the volatile oil secreted by the plant. A small number of umbelliferals including, of all things, parsley, parsnips and carrots, can have a phototoxic effect, but it is rarely severe. The invention of the strimmer has caused more problems with skin reactions than has been seen for some time. Because most men operating strimmers do so on a hot sunny day, they also are inclined to strip to the waist and so expose their torsos to a bombardment of plant material and sap, which, in the case of an umbelliferal such as cow parsley, causes a positive grapeshot effect on the skin. I have seen photographs of people who have been 'attacked' in this way and they are not a pretty sight. When using such machinery it is best to dress like a spaceman, however hot and sweaty it may be; it will be for your own good in the long run.

Allergies are more likely to affect certain allergy-prone people, and the usual safeguards apply. If you experience an allergic reaction of any kind, seek professional help immediately. Poison ivy can cause quite bad blistering and discomfort, although there is little evidence of it being widespread in this country. There have been, however, a number of recorded cases of skin reactions to this plant in the United States.

Feverfew can cause contact dermatitis. The problem of mouth ulcers is also worth mentioning but at least that can be treated successfully with tincture of myrrh.

Some of the worst cases of what might be termed herb abuse have been from the over-use of essential oils. I have read recently of two recorded fatalities in the United States from excessive use of pennyroyal essential oil in attempting home abortions. The need to use essential

oils in moderation cannot be stressed enough. They are highly concentrated forms of herbal oil and are therefore extremely powerful.

Use of Herbs in Pregnancy

Most doctors refrain from prescribing any medication, if possible, during pregnancy. Medical herbalists caution against some herbs, but are
happy to suggest absolutely safe herbs such as chamomile, psyllium
seed and dandelion, among others. However there are some herbs
which in the normal state of events are safe, but can be dangerous in
pregnancy. These are the herbs that bring on delayed menstruation and
therefore become abortifacients. The most common mentioned in this
book are: marjoram, pennyroyal, rosemary, rue, sage, tansy, thyme
and wormwood. There are others not mentioned here but they tend to
be more specialised and so more likely to be prescribed by a medical
herbalist who will not use them if there is any suggestion of pregnancy.

Do not panic over the culinary herbs used to flavour food. These will
not be present in anything like the concentrations that can cause harm.
Always consult a qualified member of the National Institute of Medical
Herbalists, recognisable by the letters MNIMH or FNIMH after their name,
or a doctor at the onset of pregnancy. This is definitely not a time for
self-medication.

Cause for Concern

In recent years a number of herbs have caused some concern among
researchers: comfrey, male fern, mistletoe and sweet flag in particular.
Although, in the case of comfrey, experiments have been conducted
using large amounts of plant material, nevertheless, until further evidence about its properties is forthcoming, it might be advisable to
refrain from using comfrey as a tisane.

In spite of such precautions, your herb garden is still a very safe
place; it is important to remember that the herbs mentioned here are
merely classed as 'hazardous'. Extensive lists drawn up by researchers
include such very ornamental plants as tulips, daffodils, nicotiana,
hyacinth and autumn crocus, and vegetables such as tomatoes and
rhubarb. Without these in our gardens life would be pretty empty.
Sensible people do not plant daffodil bulbs among the onions, nor do
they include tulip heads in salad. Just be careful, enjoy your herbs and
don't put rue near the swimming pool or by the sandpit, and above all,
teach your children the dangers as well as the pleasures of gardening;
teach them not to eat anything from the garden unless you say so.

Use of Essential Oils in Aromatherapy

The Basics

A dozen red roses can set off a romantic chain of events, and a few drops of the oil can have the same effect. In fact, oil of rose is a very versatile essence with all sorts of uses in physical and mental therapy, but while many other oils have similar uses, only a few have such a close association with romance.

Poets have sung for thousands of years about the magic of the rose. In aromatherapy, most beginners and home practitioners will have to forgo the pleasure of using this oil because of the cost. If you were thinking of buying essential oil of rose as a birthday present for an aromatic friend, pause and consider. By weight, gold is cheaper.

First a practical point: what is aromatherapy going to cost you? Luckily for those without rich admirers, most of the useful oils are affordable. Three or four people could easily spend more on a night at a restaurant than the price of setting yourself up with the Top Ten oils, and you could get two complete sets of these for the price of one phial of rose oil!

But just what is it that you are buying? For a start, a so-called essential oil is really more like a spirit-essence than an oil. Oils such as those gathered from olives or sunflowers are greasy, turgid substances which do not readily evaporate into the air. Essential oils, these essences in their little dark glass bottles, are thin, watery liquids which evaporate before your very eyes.

The technical term is volatile, and the chemical names of the myriad constituents of these volatile spirits usually end in '-of', '-ate' or '-ene', as in other volatile fluids such as alcohol, acetate and trinitrotoluene, or TNT. In other words, leave the top off your phial and next time you look the phial will be empty.

As essential oils evaporate they carry and develop their scent, but the scent is often unrecognisably strong if sniffed neat. Some essential oils can smell less like a garden of flowers than like something you would wave under the nose of a boxer to revive him after being knocked out.

You now know how to recognise an essential oil. It is not oily, it may smell so strong it makes your eyes water, and if you put a drop on a tissue the wet mark will disappear very quickly.

The other types of oils you will come across are fragrant oils and carrier oils. Fragrant oils smell pleasant, are oily and do not evaporate as

Right: **Essential oil of rose is one of the most delicious as well as one of the most expensive oils - by weight, gold is cheaper!**

fast as essential oils. They are especially made for atmospheric uses such as pot-pourri and in aroma rings. They do not have the beneficial qualities of essential oils, just the same smell, and are only for fun.

Carrier oils are the medium by which a tiny bit of essence can be made to go a long way – for example in massage. Any kind of cold-pressed, additive-free vegetable oil could be used, but you might find olive or ground-nut a bit overpowering and so, rather than raiding the kitchen cupboard, you are probably safer and better off buying professional carrier oils, also called fixed oils. You only use a very small quantity anyway, you know they are pure, and they even have limited beneficial effects in themselves which can help the essential oils to work.

Methods

USING ESSENTIAL OILS WITH WATER

If the king of aromatherapy methods is massage, the queen has to be the aromatic bath. A few drops of well-chosen essential oils, swirled into a not-too-hot bath (evaporation, remember), can relax you when you're all wound up, or can revive you when you thought that all you wanted to do was crawl away and hide.

Above: **Sweet basil, *Ocimum basilicum*, is used as a general restorative and is particularly good for dealing with respiratory ailments.**

Certain oils in the bath can ease pain, invigorate and unknot your tired and tense muscles, and give your skin a treat into the bargain. Some oils can even act positively against infections.

If you ever have the chance, try your oils in a jacuzzi – it is fun, although rather extravagant – and next time you go to a sauna take a little phial of oil with you. A few drops added to the pan of water and then splashed on the hot stones to steam can add a whole new dimension to a sauna.

You could try oil of the white birch, *Betula alba*. It is with the twigs of this tree that Scandinavians reputedly beat each other during their sauna rituals. White birch is very good for the skin and the circulation, and the aroma reminds you of after-shave of the 'leather' type, which is no coincidence because they use birch tar oil to make such products.

Another versatile water method is steam inhalation. Put a tea-towel over your head, close your eyes and breathe in the vapours from about

23cm/9in above a steaming bowl. This can be good for all sorts of nasal and chest problems, headaches and colds, and can be effective as a form of facial, although avoid this method if you have sensitive skin, since it can produce broken or 'thread' veins. It is also a convenient way of using the powers of essential oils to relieve anxiety or give yourself a quick lift when you're feeling down.

USING ESSENTIAL OILS WITH APPLICATORS

Compresses are the main way of applying oils directly to the body. Half fill a pudding basin with water — hot if you are treating muscular aches and stiffness in the joints, cold if the problem is a headache or a strained or pulled muscle. Add up to five drops of oil, soak a clean piece of cotton cloth in the solution, gently squeeze out the surplus and hold to the affected part for as long as you feel it is doing good. Renew as necessary.

Oils can also be inhaled neat, although it is best to do this with some sort of portable 'sniffer', which need be nothing more complex than a small pill bottle with cottonwool inside with a few drops of oil added. This can be carried wherever you go.

USING ESSENTIAL OILS WITH VAPORISERS

You could be really basic about this and simply fill a saucer with water, stand it on the radiator, then sprinkle in a few drops of oil. Alternatively, you could do it in style with a burner or a vaporiser. Burners come in all shapes and materials, the basic idea being to use a night-light candle to generate just enough heat to send the molecules of essential oil out into the atmosphere of the room. As long as you can wash all traces of oil off the burner before you next use it, it doesn't matter which sort of burner you have.

Another very simple but luxurious method is the light-bulb ring. These little circular troughs fit over the bulb in a table-lamp or bedside-lamp and do the same job as the burners. You can use fragrant rather than essential oils in these atmospheric ways. You only get the aroma, not the therapy, but this may not matter in most cases. In serious applications you probably would not use the light and mild atmospheric methods anyway.

These methods are best suited to creating moods, freshening the air and making the environment more attractive to friends and lovers, or to drive away unwanted insects. The aroma alone is usually sufficient in these cases. Fragrant or essential oils can be used to revive pot-pourri, and some can be dabbed neat onto the skin as perfumes, for instance geranium, patchouli and sandalwood.

USING ESSENTIAL OILS WITH MASSAGE

Aromatherapy without massage is like a holiday without sunshine – good, but nothing like as good as it should be. Massage improves the effects of the oils so that the combined result is the greater. One and one makes three when you add essential oil to massage. However, this is also the only method in aromatherapy that requires skill and the knowledge of correct technique. It is important to visit only a qualified masseur, and if your interest progresses, perhaps you could enrol yourself on a course to learn the essential skills of massage for yourself.

SOME SIMPLE COMMONSENSE RULES MUST BE APPLIED:

- Don't massage infected or broken skin.
- Don't massage someone who is not in a fit state to be massaged, such as under the influence of drink or drugs.
- Check with a general practitioner if in doubt about the interaction of any prescribed medicine with the aromatherapy oils.
- Don't massage if you are not in a fit state.

Make sure the room and the general atmosphere are suitable. This should be a relaxing, indulgent experience; it will work better in the sitting room with soft lights and sweet music rather than on the kitchen table with glaring fluorescent tubes and an insistent disco beat. Caring aroma-masseurs and masseuses often draw the curtains and use candelight, accompanied by appropriate mood music.

Just use a little oil. Adding a single drop more to the hands is much easier than trying to wipe away a highly aromatic excess oozing all over the place. A teaspoonful of carrier oil with two or three drops of essential oil should be more than enough to do a complete back massage. Understand that increasing the proportion of essential oil will not necessarily increase the effect, and indeed may even be to the detriment of the therapeutic treatment.

There are scores of carrier or fixed oils. You can get avocado or fractionated coconut if you want, but the cheapest and most widely used general purpose carriers are grapeseed and sweet almond. Similar but with other qualities are wheatgerm and jojoba, which you can add to your blend (essentials only, or essentials plus carrier) at a proportion of about 10 per cent to enrich it. Wheatgerm is especially good for facials, and it is a preservative which helps to keep your blend from deteriorating.

So: practise your carefully learned techniques, think about what you are trying to do, add some common sense, freshen up the pot-pourri, check the warmth, the lights and the music, and away you go.

Massage techniques

Massage manuals are full of French terms such as 'effleurage' and 'pettrisage'. In plain English, the five massage techniques are: stroking, patting, knuckling, squeezing and rubbing.

STROKING

You've stroked the dog or the cat and know how much they like it. Massage strokes on people have a similar but even more marked effect. Here they are somewhat more formalised and they should follow the following rules of technique:

The aroma-masseur strokes in two ways, with a pulling or a pushing motion, and either way lightly or heavily. Take the heart as the centre of the body. If the masseur is pulling or pushing towards the heart, he or she can use pressure. If stroking away from the heart, only the lightest touch should be used.

Stroking should begin and end all massage sessions, and it should be used in between the other techniques.

PATTING

This is the least used of the five. Patting with the fingertips gives light stimulation to small areas.

KNUCKLING

The hands are clenched in very light fists. Gentle circular movements are made using mainly the knuckles of the top joints of your fingers.

SQUEEZING

Squeezing and letting go, usually with both hands at once, is a powerful technique involving plenty of effort from the masseur and leaving a clear effect on the subject.

Large muscles or muscle groups need more massage input than stroking can provide – in fact, 'knead' is *almost* the right word, because the plunging, turning, squeezing, lifting and pressing actions of the bread-maker are the nearest equivalent to this deep form of massage, except here the subject is human and expecting sympathetic treatment. Slow and kindly should be your technique; no violence, please.

Above: Fennel, *Foeniculum vulgare,* has had an enormous herbal reputation since medieval times. It is mostly used for digestive problems.

RUBBING

Everybody has, without knowing it was a massage technique, used friction, or rubbing, on a cold winter's day to warm their hands up. It's the same thing in massage: the harder and faster the masseur rubs, the better the results.

Practical uses of aromatherapy

The principal actions of aromatherapy oils are:
- as relaxants
- as tonics
- for aches and pains
- for skin care
- to induce sleep
- to act as an aphrodisiac
- to create ambience

Aromatic Relaxation

Stressed? Stress is the modern disease, accepted as an inevitable part of normal life, and so we all allow stress to take its invisible but sometimes quite considerable toll on body and mind.

It may be, in a particular case, that there is little you can do about the causes of the stress, nor possibly even about the subject's ability to handle it, but you can do something to relieve the symptoms.

Aromatherapy is essentially a very gentle way to improve well-being and restore proper functioning, using natural substances whose powers were studied and respected many centuries ago.

Quite a number of essential oils are useful relaxants but several are pre-eminent among them, and these can be used singly or in combinations to suit you. This book is not going to examine the psychological roots of anybody's stress, which may indeed need to involve other forms of therapy; individuals may be predominantly depressed, or anxious, or a mixture of the two, or may confuse the two states. This book can only provide general guidelines for mood therapy for you to enlarge on. If at first you don't succeed, try another essential oil.

The oils most widely used and frequently commended for their virtues in relief of stress are those of lavender and sandalwood. Any first attempt to relax someone should begin with one of these.

Also highly commended would be patchouli, sweet marjoram and vetivert from my second group of suggested oils (see page 52), plus chamomile from my Top Ten (see page 40).

Other oils with permutations of the right qualities include clary sage, frankincense, lemongrass, petitgrain and tangerine. Ylang ylang is also on the list but perhaps should be kept for special occasions, plus rose otto and true neroli if your stress is caused by being a millionaire and you can afford them!

Blends can really be as simple or as complicated as you like, but simple ones are probably preferable. Were you to become an advanced student of aromatherapy you might investigate synergistic blends for the treatment of guilt, or conduct experiments into the best proportions of which six oils should be employed against helplessness and bewilderment. When things are as bad as that, perhaps a more fundamental, stringent treatment is required than aromatherapy's gentle benefits.

Meanwhile, you might like to deal with a case of good old-fashioned 'nerves' by using a blend of equal amounts of lavender and vetivert. Alternatively, when the mood is gloomy, try lavender, chamomile and clary sage. If the stress in your subject tends to produce tense snappishness, then treat him or her to a massage of chamomile and sweet marjoram.

Aromatic Tonics

It's a cold, grey Sunday morning in late winter. You look out of the window at the fine but persistent drizzle and, through the depressing trickle of raindrops down the glass, you see the jobs that need doing in the garden. If this scene describes your general mood, you may only be showing the occasional sort of emotional and spiritual drain that everybody feels at some time, which awaits you after struggling out of bed in the morning.

Aromatherapy is not going to bring you a sudden vision of the meaning of life, if you were wondering what on earth it was all for, but it can give you a lift and it can add some zest to your everyday life, especially if you get into the habit of using aromatherapy regularly. Then, with your spirits brightened and your senses sharpened, you may well feel up to whatever it was that was troubling you, and once you've got up there and done it, maybe it won't be so difficult next time.

If you can't get to the seaside, but you still want to experience the bracing effect of a breath of ozone, find enough time to pay a visit to your aroma box instead and look to find some or all of these essential oils. Your ingenuity should be rewarded with a totally invigorating experience which can be relied upon to brace and uplift those who are down in the mouth.

From my Top Ten (see page 40).

•eucalyptus, geranium, juniper, lemon balm or melissa, rosemary

Add, if you wish, for more interest and variety, some of these from the second shelf:

•basil, bergamot, lemon, peppermint.

For even more versatility, there are also:

•black pepper, cypress, ginger, grapefruit, orange, palmarosa.

Try cypress, geranium and grapefruit together, or eucalyptus, grapefruit and rosemary. Experiment also by adding one of the relaxer oils to two of the revivers, giving you a blend suitable for those times when you need the motivation of a pick-me-up but you also need your nerves steadying. For example, before a big occasion, try palmarosa and lemon with sandalwood, or bergamot and palmarosa with clary sage, or any of them with lavender.

Above: Lemon balm, *Melissa officinalis,* is used to cheer up tired hearts and minds and as a general pick-me-up.

Aromatics for aches and pains

There are as many pains as there are muscles and bones, and producing a comprehensive aromatherapy index for everything would require a much weightier volume than this one, and assume diagnostic skills not communicable via the written word. Aches and pains have many and complicated causes, so let us stick here to a general approach, hoping to provide some relief where there is a problem, and some flexibility and a smile where there is stiffness and a grunt and a wince. To soothe our ills, we have at our disposal aromatic baths, massage, and a little battery of oils which will make life a bit more fun than it was.

A good general kit for pain and stiffness in muscles and joints would include:

•chamomile, eucalyptus, lavender, rosemary and sweet marjoram.

More specifically, for cramp:

•chamomile, cypress, juniper and rosemary, also, sweet marjoram and tangerine.

For strains and sprains:
- ginger, lavender, rosemary, sweet marjoram.

For rheumatic and arthritic pain: especially where there is inflammation or swelling (be very gentle):
- chamomile, cypress, eucalyptus, juniper, lavender, lemon and rosemary.

Where you need relaxing warmth, use:
- black pepper, ginger, sweet marjoram

For bruises and knocks:
- geranium, lavender, rosemary, cypress.

Other oils with beneficial qualities in this area of treatment include:
- cajeput, niaouli and vetivert.

Aromatic Skin Care

This book is not going to claim that your eczema, psoriasis or chronic acne – which so far has defeated the best of modern medical science – is miraculously curable by aromatherapy. However, these conditions can be eased by using essential oils in conjunction with pharmaceutical products.

Cosmetic skin care is covered in many books on beauty treatments. Meanwhile, for the general health and care of our outermost layers we can divide quite a large number of oils into categories matching the most common, everyday complaints which may not worry the doctor but do worry the sufferer.

For skin which is dry, itchy, tired or sore, you need the soothers and healers :
- chamomile, lavender, petitgrain, sandalwood, vetivert.

For oily skin, spots and skin in need of refreshment, the antiseptics and tonics are:
- cypress, eucalyptus, geranium, juniper, lemon, rosemary.

For cuts, sores and bites, the stronger, more medicinal oils are:
- cajeput, and – especially – tea tree.

Clary sage, lemongrass, palmarosa and patchouli also have particular benefits in skin care.

Aromatic Sleep

When asked to pick their top two oils for helping people get to sleep, most of the aromatherapists around the world would probably say chamomile and sweet marjoram, with split votes for lavender, sandalwood or ylang ylang as a best third.

If you find that these oils used on their own are not doing a satisfactory job, try blending small and equal amounts – say two or three drops – of chamomile, lavender and ylang ylang, or mix lavender with vetivert, which has special qualities in this department. Other oils which you may find of help are benzoin, clary sage and petitgrain.

To go outside our range of recommended oils for once, there is an oil made from the root of a common herb called valerian which is a specific for insomnia. Valerian has a very long and noble tradition in herbal medicine and was a popular remedy for what was once called 'the vapours', a term covering a range of conditions all the way from depression to hysteria.

Valerian root was also used around Tudor times to perfume clothes, although few people would thank you for that now. Cats like the smell, however, and will roll on valerian plants in the garden. The essential oil is more pleasant than the plant but it is less widely available than some, its only real use being in insomnia and nerve-calming.

Aromatic Aphrodisiacs

Above: Sweet marjoram, *Origanum majorana*, is used for soothing aches and pains, bruises and strains.

Let's be quite clear about this. There are no secret essential oils with magic aphrodisiac qualities. There is nothing in the aroma shop which can be slipped into the lover's wine, sprinkled on sleeping eyelids or burned to perfume a boudoir, which will have the same level of effect as the princess's kiss on the frog.

Cures for unrequited love are not in the catalogue. Physical impossibilities cannot be rendered possible. Youthful performance, if long gone, cannot be conjured up. However, if there is potential, we might be able to do something.

Experts agree that only one of my Top Ten oils is an aphrodisiac, and that is ylang ylang. Some of the other Top Ten oils are commended, if not unanimously – juniper berry, rosemary and sandalwood, for example – and others have romantic attributes which can be used as part of a multi-tactic strategy.

Several of my second group of oils can be regarded in a similarly positive light to ylang ylang, for instance clary sage, ginger, and lemon. Others with general stimulant or soothing properties can be helpful in the right context.

Two oils with very firm reputations as encouragers of romantic feelings are prohibitively expensive. The rich may be able to afford rose and jasmine, but the rest of us have ylang ylang at our disposal, and fortunately there is little difference as far as results are concerned.

If you absolutely must have rose, you can make the sacrifice seem less by buying it diluted and ready for use in a carrier oil. Alternatively, you can simulate the aroma – if not the qualities – of rose with a mixture of ylang ylang and clary sage.

Recipes for romantic blending are given below. Of course, you can create your own blends, and you can alter the balance of the blends given according to special circumstances. Be careful to cross-check on the other qualities of the oils before you experiment too wildly.

Below: The Apothecary rose, *Rosa gallica,* as its name suggests, is the most widely used rose species in western medicine.

Oils to drop hints with: a little subterfuge can go a long way, such as a drop of oil carefully placed where the desired one will surely find it. Give him or her a present, but make sure there's a scrap of cotton or tissue in the packing on which you have 'accidentally' tipped a minute quantity of oil.

Next time it's the birthday of your object of desire, or Valentine's Day, don't forget the aromatic clue inside the greetings card. Because of the price, you might not want to use rose, but ylang ylang or geranium should do the job.

Aromatic Ambience

Whether it's just a drink or two in the sitting room or a lovingly prepared six-course meal, romantic inclinations can be identified and developed by a subtle atmosphere containing the most suitable aromas. A couple of bowls of delicious pot-pourri might be inkling enough, or you might want to intimate romance more emphatically with a burner.

In either case, the oils to use include benzoin, patchouli and ylang ylang. Add one of the citrus oils such as grapefruit if some waking up needs to be done, or alternatively try using sandalwood for a truly wonderful relaxing note.

Males with amorous intentions might add clary sage or black pepper. Females could try chamomile and palmarosa.

Should you be past the drinks and dinner stage and wanting simply to make sure that the bedroom is not only for sleeping, a good blend for the bedside pot-pourri uses palmarosa as the base – say 10 drops – with a couple of drops each of ylang ylang and clary sage. If you can get them, try also adding a similar amount of nutmeg and lime.

If you are exhausted by all this secret aromatic activity, feeling full after the six courses or tired and emotional after too many glasses of wine, you could consider a nice warm bath to get you back into the mood. Grapefruit, palmarosa and, again, ylang ylang suggest themselves as suitable helpers..

●Oils for close encounters: one school of thought says that it is the massage that has the effect. Romantic conclusions would, they say, inevitably follow the stroking and squeezing, even if you used a blend of virgin olive and tea tree. Such people are cynics and do not deserve magic moments. Massage, of course, is all part and parcel of aromatherapy, but it is far, far better to use a blend of oils especially designed for the purpose. As with all massage, the right essential oils with it increase the desired effect far beyond simple addition.

Make a blend of equal amounts of lemon and palmarosa, five drops each, plus a drop or two of ylang ylang. Alternatively, use tangerine as the base, with black pepper added to it.

Right: Liquorice is of value for coughs, ulcers and arthritis. But beware: in large doses it can have side effects.

●Oils to fuel the drives: if the idea is not so much to catch and kiss, but to make the already-caught want to kiss again, the classic sex drive oils are clary sage, geranium and ylang ylang, or even rose otto, if you deem it worth the expense. How you use them is up to you!

The Top Ten Oils

In alphabetical order, the top ten essential oils are:
•chamomile •cypress •eucalyptus •geranium •juniper •lavender
•rosemary •sandalwood •tea (ti) tree •ylang ylang

Of these, only chamomile is expensive, although juniper berry and the best sandalwood are also dearer than the others. This is a very basic beginner's list of safe oils which covers a variety of the most common purposes.

Chamomile

USES: as a relaxer; for aches and pains; for skin care; for helping to induce sleep.

Safe, versatile and held in highest regard for thousands of years, chamomile is one of the most important oils of all. The oil is distilled from the flowers and is middle note.

Nowadays, you will see two or even three kinds of chamomile on sale: Roman, German and Maroc. Which do you use?

Roman and German are very similar. German is less common and more expensive with a stronger blue colour. Its prime advantage over Roman is possibly some extra power against skin complaints and so it tends to be used when the severity of the complaint justifies the extra expense.

Maroc is a relative newcomer. Strictly speaking, it is not chamomile at all except by common name. It is disregarded by some experts because it does not have as many uses and may not have such a powerful effect as other types. However, it is cheaper and quite similar, and should be found effective with skin problems and as a relaxer and reliever of tensions.

Roman chamomile, *Chamaemelum nobile*, also called sweet, English, garden and true chamomile, is the one of chamomile lawn fame. It has a daisy-like flower, ferny leaves and a sharp apple scent. Chamomile is not only good for people. Also called the 'Plant Doctor', it is supposed to help the growth and well-being of the other plants in the garden just by being there.

Effective to a certain extent in all kinds of emotional and stressful conditions, chamomile is especially commended as a calming substance. When someone is particularly upset by a traumatic experience, feeling they can't cope with life, suffering with 'nerves' or stress, this oil can be

Right: A chamomile lawn is very difficult to grow successfully - instead cultivate it in small patches as it is here between the flag stones.

most helpful. Its usefulness as a calming agent combines well with its anti-inflammatory and mild pain-killing properties in such problems as infant teething troubles. Try a little chamomile in your child's bath, or in an aroma ring in the nursery.

●Suitable methods for relaxing with chamomile: water; applicators; vaporisers; massage.

Chamomile's ability to reduce inflammation is one of its most highly prized features. It is also credited with a gentle analgesic effect and so many uses can be suggested where muscles and joints are swollen and causing distress. Rheumatic and arthritic sufferers can look to chamomile for relief, as can children and adults with much more short-term complaints, such as tiredness after exertion.

Next time you walk those few extra miles further than you expected, try chamomile in a foot bath. What could be more pleasant than a chamomile massage after a vigorous work-out?

●Methods for using chamomile for aches and pains: water; applicators; massage.

Anti-inflammatory, at the same time as gentle, soothing, antiseptic, and able to give some relief from pain – this is obviously a good combination for skin which is sore from being wet and cold. Chamomile may also help with teenage spots, dry skin, windburn, sunburn, or even chronic skin conditions such as acne and psoriasis. A chamomile compress can be used to take the soreness out of a boil, a minor wound or burn, or an insect bite.

●Suitable methods for using chamomile in skin care: applicators; massage.

Along with lavender and some of my second group of oils, chamomile is one of the most frequently recommended oils for sleepless nights. It must be used sparingly, because too much can have the opposite effect. It is safe for children.

●Methods for inducing sleep: water; applicators; vaporisers; massage.

Changes in diet bring about a whole range of problems, from constipation to diarrhoea, from heartburn to flatulence. Chamomile can help in all such unpleasant situations, and while there is no known cure for a hangover, at least the world seems a less oppressive place with chamomile aromatherapy.

●Methods for easing digestive complaints: water; applicators; vaporisers; massage.

Chamomile, along with geranium from my top ten essential oils, does seem to have special properties for the relief of the pains and stresses associated in some women with periods, pre-menstrual tension and menopausal problems. Its calming and muscle-relaxing powers combine to relieve such cases.

•Methods for menstrual problems: water; vaporisers; applicators.

Roman chamomile is classed as a feminine scent. Although not widely used as a liquid ingredient by perfume manufacturers, try it by the vaporising methods or in pot-pourri to give a feminine touch.

Cypress

USES: as a reviver; for aches and pains; skin care. The oil is distilled from the twigs, needles and cones and is middle note.

Cypress is chiefly known as an astringent, deodorant, drying oil. It can also be good for circulatory, digestive and menopausal problems.

Safe and unlikely to cause any irritation, cypress oil has a very long history, going back with myrrh and frankincense to ancient Babylon. In Far Eastern tradition, cypress is considered a useful aid when fluid is the problem, such as heavy sweating, heavy loss of menstrual fluid and diarrhoea.

Cupressus sempervirens is not grown much in the United Kingdom as it requires warmer climes. You will see a lot of it in the south of France, where it is grown widely for commercial use. Cypress is widely used in men's toiletries because its 'heavy' scent can be more acceptable for men than the floral oils.

Cypress is a good mind-clearer and can help when a pick-me-up is needed, or when the brain is buzzing and you can't sleep.

•Methods for cypress as a tonic: water; vaporisers; massage.

Cypress can be used for aches and pains but, again, this is not its main use, but it can be put to beneficial use with cramps and swellings. Where poor circulation is causing the discomfort, this oil should be especially helpful.

•Methods for aches and pains: water; applicators; massage.

All essential oils are antiseptic in some way or other, but cypress is especially so. Cypress is also an astringent and can be used as a styptic to stop blood, although it is chiefly for its fragrance that perfume manufacturers use it so much in aftershave. Cypress is a skin revitaliser and freshener, and is particularly employed to combat greasy, oily skin.

•Method for skin care: applicators.

Cypress is of limited use as an aphrodisiac; it is more likely to make you think of a bracing walk in January than of romantic evenings in tropical moonlight. Nevertheless, as a general reviver, it is well worth using - and if you feel healthy and vigorous and happy, then anything becomes possible!

Eucalyptus

USES: as a tonic; for aches and pains; for skin care. The oil is distilled from the leaves and is top note.

It is widely used to combat breathing problems, both the bronchial and asthmatic sorts. Anyone who has ever had a cold will surely recognise the smell of eucalyptus. This celebrated cold treatment is one of the most powerful-smelling ingredients in chest and head-clearing ointments, inhalants and in cough sweets.

There are something like 500 varieties of eucalyptus. The one used most for commercial essential oil is *Eucalyptus globulus*, which is the famous blue gum tree of Australia.

Feeling sleepy? Don't want to feel sleepy? Few essential oils can clear the fuzz away like eucalyptus. It can also give relief on a muggy, hot day.

•Methods for eucalyptus as a tonic: water; applicators; vaporisers; massage.

Like quite a number of essential oils, eucalyptus can be helpful with general pains and swellings, but its main strength is in providing relief and respite for tired, over-worked muscles. This is the one for post-aerobic stiffening, or for pulls and strains.

•Methods for aches and pains: water; applicators; massage.

Eucalyptus is one of the stronger antiseptics among essential oils, and its cooling, anti-inflammatory, insect-repelling properties make it a natural choice for stings and bites, rashes, flushed skin and spots.

•Method for skin care: applicators.

Coughs, colds, throat infections, catarrh, 'flu, blocked sinus, asthma – all such similar constrictions and congestions can be relieved with eucalyptus. The antiseptic action may help clear away some of these conditions, and the invigorating vapours will make you feel better.

•Methods for aiding breathing: water; vaporisers; massage.

Geranium

USES: as a tonic; for skin care. The essential oil is distilled mainly from the leaves and is middle note. Geranium oil can also be very good for menopausal problems and pre-menstrual tension An extremely popular all-round oil, geranium, or more properly, pelargonium, has a scent which almost everybody finds highly attractive, though some people do find it repellant. It is a safe, uplifting, body-cleansing oil with a long tradition through its wild equivalents, herb Robert and cranesbill.

Although these have many specific uses in herbal lore, for example in cures for dandruff, sterility and peptic ulcers, geranium oil in family aromatherapy is most important for its ability to lighten the mood and to help with skin care.

Pelargonium graveolens is the geranium used for oil extraction, one of many hundreds of varieties bred from the African original since it was brought to Europe 300 years ago.

You've see those tedious television advertisements suggesting you should take such and such a pill to relieve your tense, nervous headache? Instead, use geranium oil. When the day has given you a battering and your spirits need a lift, this is the one that should be used.

•Methods for geranium as a tonic: water; applicators; vaporisers; massage.

Geranium oil is a cleansing, toning and sharpening oil and so is helpful with those problems which come with greasy, over-oily skin. It can help you deal with cold sores, chilblains and weather-beaten skin. Used as a gargle, just a couple of drops in warm water, geranium has a soothing effect on sore mouths and throats.

•Methods for skin care: water; applicators.

Geranium is classed by perfumers as both a male and a female-attracting scent and is recommended for stimulating hormone production. Some experts say it can be helpful where certain urges don't seem to be quite so urgent any more, but in any case its lively, flowery smell can only act positively in a romantic situation.

Above: An old terracotta urn adds an extra visual dimension to a garden. This one is disappearing into a sea of low-growing *Geranium macrorrhizum*.

Juniper

USES: as a tonic; for aches and pains; for skin care; as an aphrodisiac. Juniper berry oil is middle note.

This evergreen shrub is used in oil production. The superior product is the one distilled just from the berry, the same berry that is used to flavour gin. The oil is mainly regarded as a cleanser and stimulator. It was used for centuries as a household disinfectant and herbal remedies to stimulate bowel and kidney action. Along with the related cypress, and eucalyptus, this oil can be useful when detoxification is needed.

WARNING: although safe in most situations, juniper must not be used by pregnant women, especially in the early months, nor on anyone with kidney trouble. In any case it should never be used over-liberally although there will usually be no problems with a sensible approach.

This is a good pick-me-up, an uplifting oil in times of stress and anxiety. Tiredness, lassitude and general 'floppiness' can be dispelled. If you are changing your lifestyle habits and resolving to follow a healthy regime, then juniper and the New You definitely go together.

•Methods for juniper as a tonic: water; applicators; vaporisers; massage.

Used in the herbal tradition for gout, arthritis and rheumatism, juniper stimulates circulation and gives a fillip to aching muscles and creaking joints. Period pains and aching breasts can also be relieved.

•Methods for aches and pains: water; applicators; massage.

Oily skin, greasy hair, spots and tired skin should all respond well to juniper. This is a tonic, strong on the healthy glows and the feel-good factor. It is used in the toiletry industry as an ingredient in the spicier after-shaves and perfumes.

•Methods for skin care: applicators.

Juniper as a perfume ingredient is supposed to be attractive to both males and females, and some experts, although not all, use it as an aphrodisiac. More experiments are obviously needed.

Lavender

Above: French lavender, *Lavandula stoechas*, is very ornamental, but does not produce the quality of oil that old English lavender does.

USES: as a relaxant; for aches and pains; for skin care; to induce sleep. Lavender oil is middle note.

It can also be good for digestive and menstrual and menopausal problems, helpful in colds and 'flu, blocked sinuses and sore throats, and is an insect repellent.

This is the most versatile oil, the best all-rounder and the one you cannot be without. It is safe, and has been used in the herbal tradition for thousands of years as a virtual cure-all and general comforter, although especially as a pain killer, healer of wounds, and as a balancer of the spirits. Lavender is credited with both calming and uplifting powers and so can be equally prescribed as a soothing agent in anxiety and a stimulant in depression.

As with chamomile and sandalwood, the Latin name is very important for making sure that you are buying the oil from the right plant. *Lavendula angustifolia*, also called *Lavendula officinalis*, is true lavender, of which there are several species with mauve, purple or blue flowers, all of which can be used to make the oil by distillation.

Oils from spike lavender, or from lavendin – a cross between lavender and spike lavender – have wide uses similar to those of true lavender but their more medicinal, moth-ballish scent makes them far less popular both with the user and recipient!.

Our emotions can be upset in many ways, through a continuing aggravating situation such as environment problems or an on-going relationship, or a more sudden cause – sometimes immensely traumatic. The result can be to send the sufferer in the direction of hysteria and panic, or towards depressive headaches, morose lack of self-belief and a defeatist attitude. Lavender is a balancing oil, one which brings you back to normal from whichever direction, and so can be described as an energiser and a calming agent.

•Methods for lavender as a relaxant: water; applicators; atmospherics; massage.

Lavender's wonderful therapeutic qualities have always been believed to include pain relief and reduction of inflammation, and so this oil obviously suggests itself for dealing with muscular strains and shock. Stiff joints, headaches and period pains can also be susceptible to its aromatic powers.

•Methods to relieve aches and pains: water; applicators; vaporisers; massage.

This oil in the herbal tradition is said to encourage cell growth and so should be used to help with mending and regeneration in all kinds of skin ailments: bites, stings, boils, burns, stretch marks, rashes, spots, cold sores. It is also recommended against athlete's foot.

•Methods for skin care: water; applicators; massage.

When grandmother puts a few drops of lavender perfume on a handkerchief and leaves it under her pillow, she is following one of the oldest remedies for insomnia in the world. She also, without knowing it perhaps, has the dose right. You just need to use a very little of the essential oil otherwise it can begin to work as a stimulant.

•Methods for using lavender to induce sleep: water; vaporisers.

Another oil whose perfume is classified as both a male and female fragrance, lavender does not number 'aphrodisiac' among its many characteristics nor, like some, is it expected to reawaken desire.

Rosemary

USES: as a tonic; for aches and pains; for skin care; as an aphrodisiac. The flowering sprigs of rosemary are used to make the oil, which is middle note.

It can also be good for digestive problems, is helpful with impeded breathing, is an insect repellent and is highly regarded in hair care. Rosemary is one of the most important oils among our Top Ten. As long as humans have used medicine, rosemary has been employed for its antiseptic, cleansing, clearing powers and it has been claimed that it also aids memory and concentration.

Interestingly, while modern users of rosemary stalks throw them on the barbecue for extra savour, the ancient Greeks used to burn them as tributes to the gods. Medieval Europeans thought it would drive away evil spirits. Besides rosemary's range of qualities in skin care, it is also recommended particularly for getting rid of dandruff and livening up tired, dull hair.

NOTE: Although generally safe, rosemary must not be used by pregnant women, especially in the early months, nor by anyone with epilepsy.

Above: Prostrate rosemary cascading over a drystone wall in Provence. This plant just adores hot, dry conditions in full sun.

This stimulating oil works like sunshine on a misty morning, clearing away mental fogs and sharpening fuzzy minds. If you don't feel quite up to an especially busy day ahead, try a few drops of rosemary oil in the morning bath, and likewise if there's a hectic evening to enjoy after a very wearing day.

•Methods for rosemary as a tonic: water; vaporisers; massage.

Physical as well as mental uplift can be expected from rosemary and this fact, along with its mild pain-relieving and all-round enlivening effects, make it very good for aching muscles.

•Methods for aches and pains: water; applicators; vaporisers; massage.

Skin conditions which will respond to cleansing, antiseptic, astringent and stimulating action will be helped by rosemary. Where the flow of blood in the veins needs encouragement, and the skin needs a tonic, rosemary must come to mind.

•Methods for skin care: water; applicators; massage.

Rosemary was used ceremonially to represent love and death in the ancient religions, which may be why some experts give it as an aphrodisiac. Certainly it would be more useful for wakening than creating a romantic, sensual background. Rosemary is classified as a masculine scent which is attractive to females.

Sandalwood

USES: as a relaxant; for skin care; for inducing sleep. Sandalwood essential oil is base note.

It can also be good for digestive problems, and can help where coughs and bronchial infections have caused soreness.

Sandalwood is one of the great calming agents, and safe, too. The familiar rich aroma has been present in perfumes for thousands of years. The herbal tradition considers sandalwood especially effective in the treatment of ailments in the lungs and the bladder, and as a soother of digestive upsets including hiccups, heartburn and morning sickness.

According to the Bible, God spoke to King Solomon and instructed him to make his temple furniture of sandalwood, and, unfortunately, its widespread use for construction purposes has lead to its near-extinction. Sandalwood oil is also used very widely in incenses and so the scent has strong associations with ceremony, serenity and wisdom.

There are two kinds of sandalwood oil on regular sale. Proper sandalwood is made from the wood of the parasitic evergreen tree *Santalum album*. This tree, which has to be at least 30 years old to produce the oil, comes from the province of Mysore in eastern India and is the more expensive of the two because it is so rare.

West Indian sandalwood, *Amyris balsamifera*, no botanical relation, is a much cheaper, inferior substitute which is really only for burners and similar usage.

Anyone who is anxious, tense, nervy, highly strung, or worried can benefit from the deeply affecting, calming powers of sandalwood. 'Sedative' is a word which has changed its meaning from the original ('making calm, allaying, assuaging'), now signifying a strong knock-out drug. Sandalwood is a sedative in the original sense of the word.

•Methods for using sandalwood as a relaxant: water; applicators; vaporisers; massage.

This oil is chiefly a softener and a soother, so use it for dry skin, wrinkly skin, flaky skin, and where there is irritation from sunburn, nettle stings and so on. Itching and rawness, for instance from shaving or exposure to wind and rain, can be relieved with sandalwood.

•Methods for skin care: applicators; massage.

It really is one of the most attractive, well-rounded aromas to have in your bedroom. Sandalwood creates a serious, calm ambience, not a frivolous one, and this aspect of the oil may well help its natural sedative qualities towards easing troubled minds at night.

●Methods: water; vaporisers; massage.

Sandalwood is a two-sided perfume in the sexual sense, being attractive both to male and female, and is said to be able to induce passionate notions when otherwise they might not occur. Its sweet, woody balsamic scent lends itself to attractive blends in perfume manufacture and for this reason sandalwood is often used as a base note – that is, one of the long-staying ingredients – in several leading brands of men's toiletry.

Tea Tree or Ti Tree

USES: skin care. This small relative of the eucalyptus was given its name because the early settlers in Australia brewed its leaves to make a drink. Tea tree oil is distilled from these leaves, and is top note.

The Tea Tree comes from the same botanical family as allspice – which produces an oil to be used occasionally and only with great care – and eucalyptus and cajeput, both popular oils.

Tea tree has applications in the treatment of many infections. The oil is an essential for your first-aid kit. It is a very strong antiseptic, much stronger, in fact, than carbolic, yet is perfectly safe even for people prone to allergic reactions.

Like eucalyptus, it is a cleanser and a healer and had been used thus for time immemorial by the Australian aborigines before ever European settlers got hold of it.

It is the only essential oil credited by sceptics and aromatherapists alike with powers against all three invaders of human health and wellbeing: bacteria, viruses and fungi. It has no long herbal tradition in western medicine, but is the subject of considerable interest among orthodox researchers.

This oil works against the causes of infection, swelling, eruption and reducing the symptoms, so it is widely employed against sores, blisters, spots, rashes, verrucas and warts. It is also effective against discomfort of interior skin, such as mouth ulcers and sore throats, and safe enough to be employed to fight fungal infections such as vaginal thrush.

●Methods for skin care: water; applicators.

Coughs, catarrh and afflictions of the lungs and air passages; fevers; septic wounds; wherever you might use a conventional decongestant, antiseptic or cooling agent, tea tree can be your aid.

●Methods for use: water; applicators; vaporisers; massage.

Ylang ylang

USES: as a relaxant; in skin care; to induce sleep; as an aphrodisiac. You should buy only 'Extra' or 'Grade 1' oils which are from the first distillations of the flowers. The ylang ylang tree is native to Madagascar and the Philippines; it seems to be a bit of a one-off in the botanical world, and you would need the facilities and expertise of Kew Gardens to grow it in this country. The oil is widely used in the perfume industry for its exotic floral scent and its legendary aphrodisiac qualities, ylang ylang is an ingredient in some of the world's most famous and expensive concoctions.

Care has to be taken in its use. Although safe, the sheer intoxication of its scent can prove to be overwhelming and some people may feel nauseous as a result. This is a sedative oil. Anyone feeling that surge of anxiety which leads to an involuntary loss of cool can whisper 'Don't panic' to themselves as they unscrew the top of the ylang ylang.

It has excellent uses apart from the aphrodisiac. Ylang ylang is a calmer of anger and frustration and so can be employed when such emotions might otherwise spoil something important. It is supposed also to help with conditions associated with anxiety such as high blood pressure and depression. It reassures and helps build confidence.

•Methods as a relaxant: water; vaporisers; massage.

Skin care isn't its main use; may help with spots and minor ailments

•Methods for skin care: applicators; massage.

Gardens of flowers and dreamy summer scents can fill your bedroom when you sprinkle a few drops of ylang ylang on your pillow. It should also help induce a better quality of sleep, since it promotes a speedy progression to the stage of rapid eye movement (REM), when creative or therapeutic dreaming may be experienced.

•Methods: water; vaporisers; massage.

All the aromatherapy experts agree on the aphrodisiac qualities of ylang ylang, and so do the natives of the tropical Far East where it grows, among whom it is common custom to scatter the flowers on the bridal bed. It is said to work on both sexes although its strongly flowery scent makes it more feminine than masculine.

•Methods for ylang ylang as an aphrodisiac: vaporisers; massage.

The Top Ten oils listed above will provide the beginner with a basic aromatherapy set for most common purposes. In addition, you may wish to experiment with the following oils.

Secondary Oils

Basil

French or sweet basil, *Ocimum basilicum*, is the herb so popular in Italy and France for culinary use. The oil is a tonic: cooling, uplifting and restorative, and is highly regarded in the herbal tradition for its effects on respiratory ailments.

Safe, but not to be used during pregnancy, on young children, or anyone who is very ill.

Benzoin

In another form, oil of benzoin, made from the resin of the Asian tropical tree *Styrax benzoin*, is famous as friar's balsam. A balsam or balm is a healing, soothing substance, and the friar's type is especially for soothing respiratory complaints. Benzoin essential oil has this virtue, and is also good for the skin and as a warming relaxer.

It relieves stress and tension, aids depression and gives new hope to those with a sense of alienation from society. It gives confidence and helps emotional fatigue. Benzoin is a traditional ingredient in incense.

Safe, although can cause drowsiness, so do not use when driving or operating machinery. Masculine and feminine fragrance; base note.

Bergamot

If you have ever had Earl Grey tea, you will recognise oil of bergamot instantly. Made from the peel of the small, orange-like fruit of an Italian tree, *Citrus bergamia*, this is a cooling, uplifting, refreshing tonic of an oil, which is why it is frequently found in Eau de Cologne. The oil is top note. Bergamot is also useful against coughs and colds, and skin problems.

Safe, but should not be used before going into or while in sunlight because this can cause it to stain and may also cause a rash. Masculine and feminine fragrance.

Right: A cottage style herb garden can be allowed go grow delightfully informally - the herbs can be planted between traditional cottage flowers such as geraniums and columbines.

Black Pepper

As you might imagine, this oil – made from the whole peppercorns of the bush *Piper nigrum* – is the warming, rosy-glow type, so its sweet aroma can add mysterious depth to a blend. The oil is middle note.

Its main applications are for aches and pains, colds, stiffness and chills, although it is also supposed to be good for heartburn, nausea, diarrhoea and loss of appetite.

For thousands of years, Chinese and Indian doctors have been using pepper for such stomach complaints. Emotionally, it can give stamina and vitality to someone who is apathetic and lethargic. Safe, but be careful. Too much black pepper oil on the skin can cause severe irritation. Just a very little can be a masculine fragrance.

Cajeput or Cajaput

This is the cheaper, Malaysian equivalent of eucalyptus and tea tree, but definitely third in the order of merit.

It has a narrower range of uses than the other two but is a powerful antiseptic and is used as such in some dental preparations, for example gargles and throat lozenges. Cajeput is also useful for a range of skin conditions such as oily skin and spots, or insect bites. It is good for stuffiness, head colds, muscular aches and pains and arthritis. It is also useful for respiratory complaints such as asthma, bronchitis and catarrh.

Safe, although the oil may irritate sensitive skin and the mucous membranes in the nose.

Cedarwood B

This is the oil of the Virginian red cedar, *Juniperus virginiana*, the affordable near-equivalent of Cedarwood A, *Cedrus atlantica*. Cedar is a Semitic word meaning 'the power of spiritual strength', and it is for long-standing conditions such as depression that cedarwood proves most useful.

The Amerindians used their red cedar as medicine against many ailments, but especially the bronchial and rheumatic kinds.

This oil is regarded commercially as an insecticide and is good as a room freshener and insect repellent. Its ambient qualities can also be useful as an aid to meditation. Emotionally, it is useful for relaxing and soothing, or uplifting the spirits when a person is experiencing a lack of confidence.

Safe, but not to be used during pregnancy. Masculine and feminine fragrance; base note.

Citronella

Cymbopogon nardus is a lemon-scented grass, related to the lemongrass used in eastern cookery, which also provides a useful oil (*see* page 57). Citronella essential oil is a powerful insecticide and deodorant. In aromatherapy it is generally used as a freshener and stimulator; it can clear the stale fog from heads and rooms equally well.

NOTE: Generally safe but do not use in pregnancy.

Clary Sage

This is one with which to experiment carefully, not because it is toxic, but because it can do similar sorts of things to you as alcohol – and its effects can vary from person to person. It may make you feel good, it may make you feel sleepy or amorous. The oil is top note. *Salvia sclarea* makes a cooling, anti-inflammatory oil which has a wide range of uses especially in skin care and throat infections, and in nervous stress where it seems to be able both to soothe and uplift.

Do not use during pregnancy, nor when you would normally avoid alcohol, such as when driving or operating machinery. It should not be used by people who suffer from high blood pressure. It may also cause problems for some women on the contraceptive pill or hormone replacement therapy. Clary sage is classed as both a feminine and masculine scent but much more employed in men's toiletries.

Fennel

Sweet fennel is the tall, ferny, hardy herb with the aniseed flavour. Florence fennel is the close relative grown for its vegetable root: both are varieties of *Foeniculum vulgare*.

Above: Fennel is a tall, highly decorative plant as well as being useful both for culinary and medicinal use.

Modern babies have it in gripe water, and the essential oil, made from the seeds, has aromatherapy uses mostly associated with digestive problems including hiccups, nausea, flatulence and constipation. Fennel is also associated with respiratory ailments such as asthma and bronchitis as well as circulatory disorders and muscular pain.

Safe in moderation; not to be used in pregnancy or by epileptics.

Frankincense

Cynics might think that the three wise men would have been better bringing gold, fennel and myrrh, but the oil made from the resin of the frankincense tree, *Boswellia carteri*, had religious significance well before that time, as an incense and as an agent for encouraging the right atmosphere for meditating on deep matters. This property is enhanced by the fact that it deepens and slows the breath. The ancients also used it for skin diseases and as a cosmetic rejuvenator, and this is possibly one of its main virtues today. It is also useful for easing period pains. The oil is base note.

Frankincense can be good in clearing up colds and stuffiness and, allied to its old religious uses, as a calming influence in stress and anxiety. Generally safe. Appealing to both males and females.

Ginger

The uses for the essence of the root of *Zingiber officinale* are no surprise; it is a warming, stimulating, livening-up kind of oil, widely employed against aches and pains, cramps, stiffness, poor circulation and tiredness. The oil is middle note.

The old doctors also knew about its qualities as a digestive aid, and old wives would have told their daughters how quickly it gets rid of morning sickness. It's a great pity that such ordinary but truly useful knowledge is not passed on as automatically as it once was.

Generally safe, but may be slightly phototoxic to some people, that is to say that it may cause skin irritation when exposed to sunlight. Classified as a masculine and a feminine fragrance. Use with caution because oil of ginger's reputation for warming, stimulating and livening is not confined to aches and pains. Be prepared for its effects on the romantic instincts.

Grapefruit

Citrus paradisi is thought of as a fruit of the morning, a starter for breakfast because it's a tonic, because it's high in vitamin C and because it helps digestion, especially of fatty foods. Aromatherapy gives it similar attributes – a tonic for the nerves and for the skin, a help in chills and colds, and to be included in massage blends where the subject has inches to spare.

Safe, but as with other citrus oils, do not use before going into sunlight, as it may stain the skin or cause an unpleasant skin reaction. Has a shelf life of about six months. Not a commercial perfume, but its euphoric qualities may help to brighten up a jaded heart and cope with feelings of resentment and envy.

Lemon

The essential oil of *Citrus limonum* is expressed from the skin of the fruit and, like grapefruit, is a tonic high in vitamin C and is top note. The lemon has a longer and more celebrated history, however, and is very highly regarded as a medicinal power in many kinds of infection and gastric upset.

Perhaps skin care is its major use in aromatherapy; it can be used against all sorts of swellings and wounds and as a rejuvenator. It is also useful for headaches and to counteract feelings of resentment and bitterness.

Safe, although may stain the skin under ultraviolet light and/or cause a rash. Used commercially in masculine and feminine fragrances.

Lemongrass

The culinary variety of cymbopogen, *C. citratus*, is credited with rather more abilities than its relation citronella. Its background in old Indian medicine is similar – anti-fever, anti-infection – and it is an insecticide, but also is a sedative. It is a top note oil.

Helpful in skin care, for clearing heads and lungs and easing stiff muscles, this oil can additionally be beneficial with stress and nervous tension. Generally safe, although some people might find it an irritant. Masculine fragrance.

Above: A cottage garden can supply many of the herbs mentioned in this section.

Marjoram

There are two kinds of essential oil with this name – sweet marjoram (*Origanum majorana*), and Spanish marjoram, (*Thymus mastichina*). Sweet marjoram does everything the Spanish one does, such as sooth-

Above: A few choice culinary herbs can easily be grown in a windowbox where they can be readily at hand for cooking.

ing aches and pains, bruises and strains. It is also especially recommended for insomnia, and for its deeply affecting ability to smooth away troubles and comfort the poor in spirit, such as those suffering from recent grief or bereavement. Spanish marjoram or oregano is not really marjoram at all; it just smells like it.

Sweet marjoram is generally safe, but should not be used during pregnancy. While classifying it as an ingredient suitable for both masculine and feminine fragrances, perfume manufacturers may be interested to know that sweet marjoram (along with oil of hops) is supposed to be a sexual turn-off and is therefore recommended as a cure for overpowerful sex drives. The ancients believed it could console the bereaved and bring peace to the frantic, but they never prescribed it for wedding nights.

Melissa or Lemon Balm

This is the oil that cheers. Used in herbal medicine from the very beginnings of the art, one of its common names is Heart's Delight and here is where its value lies. The old doctors, knowing nothing of psychiatry but recognising melancholy, anxiety and loss of confidence, used melissa to breathe new life into a flagging spirit.

Although it also has some therapeutic value, particularly in skin and digestive disorders, oil of melissa is kept mainly as a general tonic, or specifically to help those prone to nervousness, loss of concentration, or the feeling that they are losing their battle with the world.

Safe. Lemon balm, *Melissa officinalis*, is usually sold in a form containing some citronella, lemon or lemongrass.

Myrrh

Egyptian mummies were embalmed using myrrh, but its cleansing, drying and warming properties are rather more useful these days for treating wounds, abrasions, and especially soreness in the mouth. Coughs and stuffiness can respond well to oil of myrrh, and it is said to be effective against fungal infections such as thrush and athlete's foot.

Safe but not to be used during pregnancy. Used as a base note in masculine and feminine fragrances.

Neroli or Orange Blossom

True neroli, made from the twice-yearly blossom of the Chinese orange-flower tree *Citrus aurantium amara*, is also truly expensive like rose and jasmine. Brides might consider it worth it, when they learn that this flower has a long romantic tradition linked to its emotional effects; it gives a feeling of peace although it also livens the spirits, and for this reason it was considered in many eastern folk traditions to be an essential component in wedding bouquets and bridal suite decoration.

Neroli oil is a skin tonic, and an emotional tonic too – in fact, its main employment is in relief of nervous tension, stress, including premenstrual tension, insomnia, shock and fear. It has a wonderful aroma, of course, and the distillation by-product, orange flower water, has always been a popular skin refresher, culinary ingredient and perfume.

More widely obtainable and much, much cheaper is neroli B, a blend of oils made from close relatives in the aurantia family. Generally safe, although the distilled oil may cause skin irritation. Used by perfumers in both masculine and feminine fragrances as a top note.

Niaouli

Definitely not to be confused with neroli, this is the Australian equivalent of cajeput, another antiseptic tea tree relative. It has been used by native peoples for many years as a purifier, healer and cleanser and as a warming easer of sore muscles. It is also used in respiratory conditions such as asthma, bronchitis and coughs.

Safe. The oil of *Melaleuca viridiflora* is a pharmaceutical ingredient in mouth-care and throat-care products.

Orange, Sweet

From the original Chinese native orange *Citrus sinensis* we now have navels, Jaffas, Valencias, Sevilles, and essential oil of orange. Herbal doctors use orange for chest complaints and as a stimulant for appetite and digestion. In aromatherapy too the oil is recommended for the bronchial system and for upset stomachs, but is mainly used as a tonic in depression and nervousness. It can help to enliven sallow skin.

The oil made by pressing the ripe peel – which usually comes from Brazil – is safe and of better quality than the distilled kind. There is some confusion about whether this oil can irritate the skin in sunlight like some of the other citrus oils do, so use with care. Classed as a masculine fragrance; top note.

Palmarosa

A relative of lemongrass and citronella, palmarosa – *Cymbopogon martini* – is very good for moisturising the skin and encouraging a bright and lively complexion.

It is also valued as an appetite stimulant and a tonic for tired spirits, being a gentle, comforting oil. Its cooling quality can counteract feelings of anger and jealousy. Safe. Feminine fragrance; middle note.

Patchouli

The aroma evokes tropical spices, warmth and calm, and one of its most commonplace uses is as a fragrance for bed linen where it has a dual function, acting as a stimulant to the creative urges as well as a stay-freshener. In aromatherapy it is mainly commended for skin care, both to treat damaged and tired skin and to prevent infection, and for the easing of stress. In the herbal tradition, *Pogostemon cablin*, or patchouli, is used to treat headaches and stomach complaints.

Safe. Base note in both masculine and feminine fragrances.

Right: Mint provides menthol - an essential oil which has cooling and invigorating properties.

Peppermint

Digestion, anything to do with coughs and colds, nausea, including morning sickness and, of course, minty freshness – these have been the work of peppermint for ever and a day. *Mentha piperita* is true peppermint. *Mentha arvensis,* cornmint or peppermint B, is a slightly cheaper substitute with a higher menthol content. Classed as a top note, masculine fragrance.

If you can disassociate yourself from the toothpaste tube and the chewing gum packet, oil of peppermint can also be helpful as a cooling, invigorating agent and where muscles and skin need an oil with cleansing and anti-inflammatory properties.

Emotionally, the oil combats fatigue and aids clear thinking. It may also provide a calming effect to those suffering from feelings of anger, nervousness or shyness. Generally safe, although it contains a lot of menthol, which can irritate some skin types.

Some authorities suggest it should be avoided during pregnancy and while breast-feeding.

Petitgrain

Widely thought of as a much cheaper substitute for neroli and made from the leaves and twigs of the same tree, *Citrus aurantium amara,* petitgrain is mainly employed in aromatherapy as a soothing agent in skin care, stress and insomnia.

It should also be considered in cases where the objective of the aromatherapy is to restore the body or emotions to their normal equilibrium, as for example in convalescence or any kind of general shock or jolt to the system.

Safe. A top/middle note in feminine and masculine fragrances but probably more masculine; an ingredient in several of the world's best-selling men's toiletries.

Rosewood

Distilled from the Amazonian hardwood tree *Aniba rosaedora,* this is a mild, general purpose oil for which most home therapists could easily find a substitute. Buy lavender oil for your aroma box instead of rosewood and do your bit for the rainforest. Rosewood is also available in synthetic form, which is used in cosmetic skin care, for minor wounds and for colds and coughs.

Safe. Masculine and feminine fragrance, middle/top note.

Tangerine

Often used with children, the elderly and pregnant women because of its safe and mild action in digestive complaints, especially those common physical disorders which have nervous origins such as hiccups. Tangerine is also good for jumpiness. Tangerine and mandarin oils are recommended for calming functions: sleeplessness, nervous tension and muscular cramps and spasms.

Generally safe, although like other citrus oils, may cause skin irritation, especially when exposed to sunlight. Mandarin, *Citrus reticulata*, is more frequently used in commercial perfumery than tangerine, *Citrus madurensis*. Both are masculine and feminine fragrance, middle/top note.

Vetivert

Deeply relaxing, soothing and smoothing, this essence of the roots of *Vetiveria zizanoides*, which is related to lemongrass, has the highest reputation for bringing about tranquillity where there was storm, and sleep where there was restlessness.

It has physical uses too, relaxing and easing tired and tense muscles and as a gentle help with skin roughness and soreness.

Safe. Its woody, smoky base note is included in both masculine and feminine fragrances.

Index